International Longshoremen's and Warehousemen's
Union, Local 12 v. N L R B U.S. Supreme Court
Transcript of Record with Supporting Pleadings

NORMAN LEONARD, ARNOLD ORDMAN

International Longshoremen's and Warehousemen's Union, Local 12 v. N L R B

Petition / NORMAN LEONARD / 1967 / 447 / 389 U.S. 846 / 88 S.Ct. 104 / 19 L.Ed.2d 113 / 8-2-1967

International Longshoremen's and Warehousemen's Union, Local 12 v. N L R B

Brief (P) / ARNOLD ORDMAN / 1967 / 447 / 389 U.S. 846 / 88 S.Ct. 104 / 19 L.Ed.2d 113 / 8-29-1967

International Longshoremen's and
Warehousemen's Union, Local 12 v. N L R B U.S.
Supreme Court Transcript of Record with
Supporting Pleadings

Table of Contents

In the Supreme Court

OF THE

United States

Office-Supreme Court, U.S.
F I L E D
AUG 2 1967
JOHN F. DAVIS, CLERK

OCTOBER TERM, 1967

No. 447

INTERNATIONAL LONGSHOREMEN'S AND WARE-
HOUSEMEN'S UNION, LOCAL 12,

Petitioner,

VS.

NATIONAL LABOR RELATIONS BOARD,

Respondent.

PETITION FOR A WRIT OF CERTIORARI
to the United States Court of Appeals
for the Ninth Circuit

NORMAN LEONARD,
1182 Market Street,
San Francisco, California 94102,

Counsel for Petitioner.

GLADSTEIN, ANDERSEN,
LEONARD & SIBBETT,
1182 Market Street,
San Francisco, California 94102,

Of Counsel.

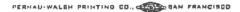

Subject Index

Table of Authorities Cited

Statutes

In the Supreme Court

OF THE

United States

OCTOBER TERM, 1967

No.

INTERNATIONAL LONGSHOREMEN'S AND WARE-
HOUSEMEN'S UNION, LOCAL 12,

Petitioner,

vs.

NATIONAL LABOR RELATIONS BOARD,

Respondent.

PETITION FOR A WRIT OF CERTIORARI
to the United States Court of Appeals
for the Ninth Circuit

International Longshoremen's and Warehousemen's
Union, Local 12, petitions for a Writ of Certiorari to
review the judgment of the United States Court of
Appeals for the Ninth Circuit, enforcing an order of
the National Labor Relations Board directed against
petitioner.

OPINION BELOW

The opinion of the Court of Appeals (R. 44-53), as modified on rehearing (R. 59), has not yet been reported. It is appended hereto as Appendix A. The Board's Decision and Order are reported at 155 NLRB 1042.

JURISDICTION

The judgment of the Court below (R. 54-57) is dated and was entered on May 9, 1967, and the petition for rehearing was denied on May 18, 1967 (R. 58-59). The judgment is appended hereto as Appendix B. The jurisdiction of this Court is conferred by 28 USC Sec. 1254 and by 29 USC Sec. 150(e).

QUESTIONS PRESENTED

The judgment below enforced an order of the National Labor Relations Board, directing petitioner to cease and desist from discriminating in the hire and tenure of employment of three named individuals and to make them whole for any loss of pay which they may have suffered by reason of the alleged discrimination.

The questions presented are:

(1) Whether substantial evidence on the record, considered as a whole, supports the Board's findings

that petitioner had committed an unfair labor practice.

(2) Whether the creation of a disruption in a dispatching hall jointly operated by an employers' association and a union is the exercise of a right guaranteed by Section 7 of the National Labor Relations Act.

(3) Whether the decision below, in its back pay aspects, conflicts with the decision of the United States Court of Appeals for the Second Circuit in *National Labor Relations Board v. Local 2 of the United Association of Journeymen and Apprentices of the Plumbing and Pipefitting Industry of the United States and Canada, AFL-CIO*, 360 F. 2d 428 (2 Cir., 1966).

(4) Whether the decision below, in refusing to give effect to the no-strike provision of the applicable collective bargaining contract, is in conflict with the earlier decision of the Court below in *National Labor Relations Board v. Tanner Motor Livery, Ltd.*, 349 F. 2d 1 (9 Cir., 1965), and with the national labor policy as expressed in Section 9 of the National Labor Relations Act.

STATUTES INVOLVED

The relevant provisions of sections 7, 8, 9 and 10 of the National Labor Relations Act, as amended, 61 Stat. 136, 73 Stat. 519, 29 USC 151, et seq., are set forth in Appendix C to this petition.

STATEMENT OF THE CASE

The Court below, exercising its jurisdiction pursuant to Section 10(e) of the National Labor Relations Act, as amended, ordered enforced a Decision and Order of the National Labor Relations Board (R. 18-31, 35-36)[1] directing petitioner to desist from engaging in an alleged unfair labor practice and ordering petitioner to make whole three named individuals for loss of wages allegedly resulting from the alleged unfair labor practice.

Petitioner is a local of the International Longshoremen's and Warehousemen's Union (which was not made a party to this proceeding). The ILWU and the Pacific Maritime Association are parties to a collective bargaining contract (U. Ex. 2), which provides that the hiring of longshoremen shall be through dispatch halls operated by joint union-employer committees (U. Ex. 2, page 64; Section 17.121). These committees are given the power to investigate and adjudicate grievances in connection with the operation of dispatch halls (U. Ex. 2, page 64; Sections 17.121 and 17.124). The collective bargaining contract also provides that *individuals* claiming to be aggrieved by the action of the parties to the contract may prosecute grievances thereunder (U. Ex. 2, pages 69-70; Sections 17.4 and 17.42), that during the life of the contract there shall be "no strike, lockout, or work stoppage" (U. Ex. 2, page 51, Section 11.1) and that

[1] References to the pleadings are designated "R." References to the stenographic transcript of the hearing are designated "Tr." References to the General Counsel's and the Union's exhibits are designated "G.C. Ex." and U. Ex.", respectively.

"the Union . . . shall be required to secure observance of this Agreement" (U. Ex. 2, page 51, Section 11.2).

The dispatching hall involved in this case is located in the little town of Coos Bay, Oregon, into which an occasional vessel calls. In addition to the registered longshoremen who serve the needs of the port, "casual men" sometimes are able to pick up an extra day or two of work. The three men involved in this case, Bernard Warnken, Lee Thomas, and Donald Wilson, are in this casual category. They had only recently come to the waterfront (Tr. 96) and had businesses of their own or other jobs on which they primarily relied (Tr. 114). They resorted to the waterfront whenever they felt like picking up a few extra dollars (Tr. 115). Unlike registered men, they had no obligation to work if they chose not to (Tr. 69).[2]

This case arose because these three casuals "didn't like the method of hiring casuals" (Tr. 36). In August of 1964, they complained to Armstrong, a working longshoreman who was the unpaid president of petitioner, that longshoremen's sons home from college on weekends were allegedly being dispatched ahead of them (Tr. 37-123). Armstrong said that he didn't know what he could do about it because dispatching was in the hands of the dispatcher, an employee of the Joint Labor Relations Committee (Tr. 38). The

[2]There apparently was great competition for the extra money cum freedom which this casual work provided. Thus in the fall of 1964 there were only fourteen days of such work a month to be spread out over 400 casuals (Tr. 121) and of the 274 casuals who actually applied for permits in 1964, only 16 were granted (Tr. 145).

contract makes the dispatcher the agent of, and responsible to, only the Joint Labor Relations Committee (U. Ex. 2, page 44; Section 8.23).

The three thereupon picketed the dispatch hall briefly (Tr. 39) and upon the advice of a PMA representative (Tr. 45, 47) presented a written grievance (G.C. Ex. 4) to the Joint Labor Relations Committee. As a result of a meeting with the Committee (Tr. 50), they were told to go back to work, that the picketing would not be held against them, and that the Committee would look into the matter (Tr. 51).

They returned to the hall and they were dispatched to such jobs as were available. However, apparently still dissatisfied, they sent another letter of complaint (G.C. Ex. 3). In a reply, dated September 29, 1964 (G.C. Ex. 5), they were assured that their complaints were "of grave concern"; that the Joint Labor Relations Committee had the "duty and obligation" to "guarantee" the proper operation of the dispatch hall; and that the matter was being investigated and would be taken care of. Instead of waiting for the Committee to resolve the controversy, they took self-help on October 8, 1964, in the form of causing a disruption in the dispatch hall (Tr. 170-174, 180-185).[3] Because of this the dispatcher lost his composure (Tr. 181-182)[4] and evicted them from the dispatch hall for

---

[3]"Well, I was upset because they were disrupting the hiring. They were waving and saying 'Plenty of work', and they were motioning to the fellows back of the other casuals there . . . 'Go on up to the window; there's plenty of work' " (Tr. 170).

[4]"I just didn't like the idea of their disrupting the hiring procedures. It's bad enough to hire people out there when you got all those hungry faces looking at you without people rushing up to the window" (Tr. 182).

that day. They thereupon resumed picketing and stayed out of the hall, thereby making themselves unavailable for work for about a month.

While the Joint Labor Relations Committee was considering their grievance at its very next meeting, the union members were served with the unfair labor practice charges filed by the three in this case. Thereupon, although the union members insisted upon going forward with the grievance under the contract (Tr. 141, 147-148), the employer members refused to proceed any further.

The three did not file any charges against the employer and the only complaint which the General Counsel issued was against Local 12. After a hearing, the trial examiner rendered a decision adverse to petitioner and, subsequently, the Board entered its Decision and Order. The Court below ordered the enforcement thereof and this Petition for Certiorari follows.

REASONS FOR GRANTING THE WRIT

I. SUBSTANTIAL EVIDENCE ON THE RECORD CONSIDERED AS A WHOLE DOES NOT SUPPORT THE BOARD'S FINDINGS THAT RESPONDENT COMMITTED UNFAIR LABOR PRACTICE.

While the Court below purported to have read the record in the light of *Universal Camera Corporation v. National Labor Relations Board*, 340 US 474 (1951),[5] the fact is that it could not have done so,

---

[5] "The substantiality of evidence must take into account whatever in the record fairly detracts from its weight." (340 US at 488). See *Filler Products Inc. v. National Labor Relations*

because the record does not support the Board's findings.

A. The record does not show a violation of 8(b)(1)(A).

Section 8(b)(1)(A) makes it an unfair labor practice for a labor organization to restrain or coerce employees in the exercise of their rights under Section 7 of the Act. That Section gives employees the right to engage, or refrain from engaging, in concerted activities for their mutual aid and protection. The record must, therefore, establish, according to the *Universal Camera* standards that, (1) the labor organization restrained or coerced employees and, (2) did so because the employees were engaged in protected concerted activities. This record does not support findings with respect to either of these two points.

First, there is no showing that Local 12 restrained or coerced any of the three charging parties, even if they be deemed to be "employees"—a dubious proposition at best in view of their casual status, supra, p. 5. After the initial picketing they returned to the hall and were dispatched. Their grievance was in the process of orderly adjudication. They were not told to stay away from the hall *until after they had created a disturbance therein.* (Compare *Pacific Maritime Association and John A. Mahoney,* 140 NLRB 9 [1962].) Thereafter, and during the second picketing, they stayed away from the hall and thereby made

---

Board, 376 F. 2d 369, 372-373 (4 Cir., 1967); *National Labor Relations Board v. Purity Food Stores, Inc.,* 376 F. 2d 497, 501 (1 Cir., 1967); *Rives Manufacturing Corp. v. National Labor Relations Board,* 376 F. 2d 511, 515 (6 Cir., 1967).

themselves unavailable for work for almost a month. They returned at a slack time of the year when, the record shows, that few, if any, casuals were dispatched. The record is uncontradicted that *work dropped off significantly and substantially in the last quarter of 1964* (Tr. 155, 178). Thus the dispatcher testified without contradiction in response to questions put by the trial examiner:

> "Trial Examiner: Just a moment, please, Mr. Oldland. I want to get your best recollection of this matter and I will try to make my questions clear. In the last quarter of 1964, was there any difference with respect to work by the casuals as contrasted with the other three quarters?
>
> A. Yes, there was.
>
> Trial Examiner: And how did that go—what was the difference?
>
> A. Well, in the first three quarters, of course, we had—we always had a certain amount of slack times but we had upwards of 75, 100—maybe some days, 110 casuals out at different times, when we had the gangs all working; and after about the middle of August, it dropped down there and I think the average was around 20 some per day. There was day in and day out that we didn't have any out at all." (Tr. 160).

Furthermore, rather than showing that petitioner restrained and coerced the casuals, the record shows that petitioner's officers were sympathetic to their plight. Armstrong told the charging parties to go ahead and picket and acknowledged that he knew "how tough it was to be a casual" (Tr. 168). The union members of the Joint Labor Relations Committee sought to process the grievance in the face of PMA opposition.

This record therefore does not support a finding of the specific documentary motivation which is necessary to sustain a finding of an 8(b)(1)(A) violation.

In *Iron Workers Local 433 and Darwin W. Nyman*, 151 NLRB 1092 [1965], the Board said:

"However, the issue here is not one of general fairness, but of specific discriminatory motivation in three instances. It may be that a more precise operation would even have produced different results, but in none of the incidents under scrutiny do we note such deviation from the general mode of operation that an inference of discrimination based on such deviation alone would be warranted. . . ." (at 1100).

Furthermore, the isolated character of the dispatcher's act (compare *Perl Pillow Company and International Union of United Brewery Workers*, 152 NLRB 332 [1965]) and the fact that, if anything, it was the result of a personal loss of composure (Tr. 181-182) demonstrate that no findings of specific discriminatory motivation can be made.

Second, the activity in which the charging parties were engaged at the time they were asked to leave the dispatch hall is not an activity protected by Section 7 of the Act. Independently of the fact that there is no substantial evidence, under the *Universal Camera* standard to sustain the Board's finding on this phase of the 8(b)(1)(A) charge, it is clear as a matter of law that the conduct engaged in by the charging parties is not of a kind protected by the statute. This separate issue of law is developed in point II, infra.

B. The record does not show a violation of 8(b)(2) and there can be no order for back pay.

Section 8(b)(2) makes it an unfair labor practice for a labor organization to cause, or attempt to cause, an employer to discriminate against an employee in violation of Section 8(a)(3). Section 8(a)(3) prohibits employer discrimination against employees "to encourage or discourage membership in any labor organization". Thus in order to establish a violation of Section 8(b)(2), it is necessary that the evidence show, under *Universal Camera* standards, that, (1) the labor organization caused, or attempted to cause, an employer to discriminate against an employee for (2) the purpose of encouraging or discouraging membership in the labor organization.

There is no evidence which could conceivably support an 8(b)(2) finding. Nothing at all shows that Local 12 did encourage, or could have encouraged, PMA to violate the Act, or that PMA did so. PMA refused, on its own, to proceed with the grievance, after it learned that the charges here had been filed. The union sought to pursue the grievance but PMA, *contrary to the union's wishes,* would not do so. Certainly it cannot be spelled out from this that the union compelled PMA to do anything. Since there is no charge or complaint that PMA violated the Act, it is not seen how it can be claimed that Local 12 did so (compare *Local Union No. 12, United Rubber, etc., Workers and The Business League of Gadsden,* 150 NLRB 312, 316 n. 4 [1964]).

There is certainly no evidence that any action was taken to encourage or discourage membership in any labor organization or that these three casuals were disadvantaged in any way because of their failure to be or to become members of the union.

Since there is no 8(b)(2) violation, there can be no order for back pay against the local union. The only provision in the Act which authorizes the Board to issue a back-pay order is found in Section 10(b):

> "... back pay may be required of the employer or labor organization, as the case may be, responsible for the discrimination suffered by [the employee] ..."

"Discrimination" is used as a word of art and appears in the operative portions of the statute *only* in Section 8(b)(2). Since the record considered as a whole does not support a finding of discrimination in this statutory sense, then, even though an order of "reinstatement"[6] and to post notices might stand, a back-pay order could not.

In addition, considering the casual nature of the charging parties' employment, the Board's own observations in *United Furniture Workers of America and Colonial Hardwood Flooring Company, Inc.,* 84 NLRB 563 [1949], are pertinent:

> "An award of back pay here would be in the nature of damages to the employee for an inter-

---

[6]It is hard to understand to what these casual workers are to be "reinstated".

ference with his right of ingress to the plant, as contrasted with compensation to him for losses in pay suffered by him because of severance of or interference with the tenure or terms of the employment relationship between him and his employer in the ordinary case in which back pay is awarded and to which Section 10(c) of the Act has been held for many years to refer. The Act contains *no* provision authorizing the Board to require damages or back pay of a labor organization under such circumstances. Nor is there any legislative history that could impel a conclusion that such awards are authorized. We therefore find that the Board lacks power to grant the remedy requested by the Company in this case." (at 565-6; italics in original)

See also:

Progressive Mine Workers v. National Labor Relations Board, 187 F. 2d 298 [7 Cir., 1951].

II. THE CREATION OF DISRUPTION IN A JOINTLY OPERATED DISPATCH HALL IS NOT AN ACTIVITY PROTECTED BY SECTION 7 OF THE ACT.

Section 7 of the Act provides that employees shall have the right "to self-organization, to form, join, or assist labor organizations, to bargain collectively through representatives of their own choosing, and to engage in other concerted activities for the purpose of collective bargaining or other mutual aid or protection, and shall also have the right to refrain from any and all of such activities . . ."

It is not, as a matter of law, part of the rights embraced within Section 7 to cause or participate in a disruption in a jointly operated dispatch hall, such as is revealed by this record (see page 6, notes 3 and 4, supra). In *Pacific Maritime Association and John A. Mahoney*, 140 NLRB 9 [1962], the Board dealt with a similar occurrence which had taken place in the ILWU-PMA dispatch hall in Seattle in 1957. The trial examiner found and the Board adopted his finding without change, that

> "PMA has . . . a coast wide policy of trying to maintain a peaceful waterfront and of protecting its hiring facilities from disorder, and the dispatch personnel stationed there from violence or fear of it. One may reasonably conclude that the thrust of its deregistration action against Mahoney in March 1961 was to apply that policy. Certainly, that conclusion is at least as consistent with the evidence as a belief that it had any of the ulterior motives the General Counsel attributes to it, and if that is the situation, the General Counsel has failed to carry the burden of proving his case by evidence of preponderant weight." (140 NLRB at 17-18)

Certainly, ILWU and its Local 12, the petitioner herein, are equally entitled to the same protection against disruptive activities, as was PMA in the *Mahoney* case.[7]

This must be all the more so since, at the very time the charging parties caused the disruption, Local 12 was seeking a resolution of the controversy

---

[7] In the *Mahoney* case, only PMA was named as respondent; here only Local 12. But the principles of law are, it is submitted, equally applicable to both parties to the collective bargaining contract.

through the peaceful use of the grievance machinery. Compare *NLRB v. Tanner Motor Livery, Ltd.,* 349 F. 2d 1 (9 Cir., 1965) in which the Court below held that this circumstance alone required a remand of the case to the Board, not the enforcement of its order.

III. THE DECISION IN THIS CASE IS CONTRARY TO THE DECISION OF THE COURT OF APPEALS FOR THE SECOND CIRCUIT IN NATIONAL LABOR RELATIONS BOARD v. LOCAL 2 OF THE UNITED ASSOCIATION OF JOURNEYMEN, ETC., 360 F. 2d 428 (2 CIR. 1966).

In the *Local 2* case, supra, the Court of Appeals for the Second Circuit modified a Board back-pay order which did not appear to contemplate an inquiry into the length of time the employer would have kept the charging parties at work.

The Court said:

"The right to back pay is not a punitory award for having been the victim of an unfair labor practice; it rests on the right to have had the work and presupposes the ability to do it. To award a man 'wages which he could not have earned would not be remedial but punitive' (Chairman Farmer, concurring, in Local 57, International Union of Operating Engineers, 1954, 108 NLRB 1225, 1230). See N.L.R.B. v. U. S. Truck Co., 6th Cir. 1942, 124 F. 2d 887, 889-890; N.L.R.B. v. Waterfront Employees, 9th Cir. 1954, 211 F. 2d 946, 953; N.L.R.B. v. R. K. Baking Corp., 2d Cir. 1959, 273 F. 2d 407, 411; N.L.R.B. v. Ozark Hardwood Co., 8th Cir. 1960, 282 F. 2d 1, 8; The Red River Lumber Co., 1939, 12 NLRB 79, 89-90; Empire Worsted Mills, 1943, 53 NLRB

683, 690-692 (award approved, 2d Cir. Feb. 14,
1944); Roskam Baking Co., 1964, 146 NLRB 15,
17-18; cf. N.L.R.B. v. Mastro Plastics Corp., 2d
Cir. 1965, 354 F. 2d 170, 175; N.L.R.B. v. Dazzo
Products Inc., 2d Cir. 1966, 358 F. 2d 136. Para-
graph 2(b) of the Board's order must be modified
to permit inquiry in the compliance proceeding
into the length of time for which, but for the
Union's activities, the four men, on the basis of
their ability and other factors, would have been
kept at work by Astrove." (360 F. 2d at 434.)

Here, since the men were casuals, called the tape
whenever they desired, worked only if they desired
and only when work was available, the order must be
modified to permit inquiry into these questions as they
relate to the matter of back pay, all as required by
the Court of Appeal's decision in the *Local 2* case.

The Court below was of the view that the Board
order in the instant case "contemplates" such an inquiry (R. 52). In fact, nothing in the order here
contemplates such an inquiry and this order is indis-
tinguishable from the one modified by the Second
Circuit in the *Local 2* case. There the order required
that the union "make whole [four named individuals]
in the manner indicated in the remedy section of this
Decision, for all losses in pay sustained by reason of
their being deprived of employment by Astrove [the
employer] . . .". *Local Union No. 2 of the United Association, Etc. v. Jose Rodriguez, et al.,* 152 NLRB
1093, 1115 (1965). The Second Circuit directed that
that order be modified by inserting after the words
"pay sustained" the words "for the length of time

for which, but for the Union's activities, the four men, *on the basis of their ability and other factors*, would have been kept at work by Astrove . . ." (360 Fed. 2d at 436; italics supplied).

The Board order contains no such limitations (R. 35, 29-30) and the refusal of the Court below to require one results in a direct conflict between the decision below and that of the Second Circuit.

IV. **THE DECISION IN THIS CASE IS IN CONFLICT WITH THE NATIONAL LABOR POLICY EXPRESSED IN SECTION 9 OF THE NATIONAL LABOR RELATIONS ACT.**

By virtue of Section 9 of the Act, ILWU and its Local 12, petitioner herein, were "the exclusive representatives of all the employees" using the Coos Bay Dispatching Hall. As such, petitioners had the right and duty to administer the no-strike and grievance arbitration provisions of the collective bargaining contract (supra, page 4), and to that extent legally to affect the rights guaranteed to the charging parties by Section 7 of the Act (*National Labor Relations Board v. Lundy Mfg. Corp.*, 316 Fed. 2d 921, 925 [3 Cir., 1963]), even assuming that creating a disruption in a dispatch hall is such a right (see point II, supra). Petitioner, or its parent ILWU, might well be held liable in damages for actions of the charging parties which breached those provisions of the contract. *Atkinson v. Sinclair Refining Co.*, 370 US 462 (1962).

While it is true that Section 9 gives to individual employees the right to have grievances adjusted without intervention of the bargaining agent, it has been held that this right does not include the right to picket in protest against an employer's hiring policy in the face of a grievance procedure through which such issues could be raised. *National Labor Relations Board v. Tanner Motor Livery, Ltd.,* 349 Fed. 2d 1 [9 Cir., 1965].

The Court below held that the no-strike provision of the contract was not applicable because the "picketing and other activities" of the charging parties did not constitute "a strike or work stoppage against one or more employers" (R. 52). If this means that there was no violation of the no-strike clause because three individuals were not "employees" as the cases which the Court below cites all indicate,[8] then the Act is not applicable to them at all since Section 7 applies only to "employees". If the Court meant that the picketing and causing disruption (which the Court calls "other activities") at a jointly operated dispatch hall is not conduct directed against "one or more employers", it simply misread the record which demonstrates that the dispatch hall is operated jointly with the employers and is the place at which "one or more employers" obtain their labor force and is precisely the point at which a strike or work stoppage directed against employers would occur.

The Court says that the question of the availability of the grievance procedure was not properly before it

[8]*National Labor Relations Board v. Illinois Bell Telephone Co.,* 189 Fed. 2d 124 (7 Cir., 1951); *The Point Reyes,* 110 Fed. 2d 608 (5 Cir., 1940); and *C. G. Conn Ltd. v. National Labor Relations Board,* 108 Fed. 2d 390 (7 Cir., 1939).

because it asserts, erroneously, that the issue was not raised before the Board (R. 52-53). To the contrary, the record before the trial examiner shows that the question of grievance procedure and its exhaustion in lieu of taking other action was thoroughly covered (see e.g., Tr. 47, 50-1, 59-60, 77-8, 83 [cross-examination established the failure to exhaust available grievance machinery]; Tr. 84-5, 90-1, 103-5, 137-9, 140, 141 [petitioner took position that the three casuals were entitled to have their grievances processed under the contract]; Tr. 146-8, 150-1 [the issue of the grievance machinery was just about the only testimony from defense witnesses]). In its briefs to both the trial examiner and the Board, respondent asserted:

"... instead of waiting for the Joint Labor Relations Committee procedure to resolve the controversy, they took self-help in the form of causing a disruption in the dispatching hall ... In the meantime, the Joint Labor Relations Committee was investigating the alleged grievance ... and while considering it at its next meeting, the union members thereof were served with the unfair labor practice charges in this very case. Thereupon, the employer members refused to proceed any further ..."

The trial examiner's decision contains a complete discussion of this matter and shows that the issue was raised (R. 21, 23, 24). The respondent's very first exception to the trial examiner's decision was to its failure to find that respondent's president had advised the casuals "that the Joint Labor Relations Committee, not the union, had the responsibility for correcting grievances relating to dispatching" (R. 32).

Therefore, contrary to the opinion, this question was in fact presented to the agency.

In any case, the decision of the Court below in *National Labor Relations Board v. Tanner Motor Livery, Ltd.*, 349 Fed. 2d 1 (9 Cir., 1965) was not published until after September of 1965, when the exceptions to the trial examiner's report were filed and, therefore, if there was a failure initially to raise the point as sharply as it was raised after that decision, that failure is clearly excusable under the provisions of Section 10(c) of the Act.

The importance of the issue—strike and disruption against orderly use of available grievance machinery —requires resolution here since the Court below refused to deal with the problem.

CONCLUSION

For each of the foregoing reasons, the Writ of Certiorari should be granted and the judgment below reversed.

Dated, San Francisco, California,
        July 20, 1967.

Respectfully submitted,
NORMAN LEONARD,
        Counsel for Petitioner.

GLADSTEIN, ANDERSEN,
    LEONARD & SIBBETT,
        Of Counsel.

(Appendices Follow)

Appendices.

United States Court of Appeals
For the Ninth Circuit

National Labor Relations Board,
                              Petitioner,

vs.

International Longshoremen's and Warehousemen's Union, Local 12,
                              Respondent.

No. 20,914

[April 18, 1967]

On Petition to Enforce an Order of the
National Labor Relations Board

Before: Chambers and Hamley, Circuit Judges, **and**
        Byrne, District Judge

Hamley, Circuit Judge:

The National Labor Relations Board (Board) petitions for enforcement of its order of November 18,
1965, issued against respondent, International Longshoremen's and Warehousemen's Union, Local 12.
The Board decision and order is reported at 155
N.L.R.B. No. 89.

The Board's regional director alleged in his complaint that Local 12 had engaged in unfair labor
practices in violation of section 8(b)(1)(A) and 8

(b)(2) of the National Labor Relations Act (Act), 49 Stat. 452, as amended, 29 U.S.C. § 158(b)(1)(A) and (2) (1964). Local 12 had violated these statutes, it was alleged, by failing to dispatch Donald Wilson, Bernard Warnken and Lee Thomas, the charging parties, from the dispatch hall, and by excluding them from the dispatch hall. The trial examiner entered findings and conclusions upholding the charges and upon agency review, the Board adhered to the trial examiner's findings and conclusions.[1]

The Board order requires Local 12, together with its officers and agents, to cease and desist from the specified unfair labor practices. It also requires them to make Wilson, Warnken and Thomas whole for loss of pay suffered by reason of such practices. In addition, the order contains the usual provisions concerning the posting of notices and the giving of notifications.

Wilson, Warnken and Thomas worked out of North Bend-Coos Bay, Oregon, longshoremen's dispatch hall. The hall was established pursuant to a collective bargaining agreement between the International Longshoremen's and Warehousemen's Union (ILWU), of which Local 12 is an affiliate, and an association of employers known as the Pacific Maritime Association (PMA). Under the terms of that agreement, the hall, which offers the only means longshoremen have of obtaining work in that area, is governed

---

[1] The Board order modifies, in certain respects, the trial examiner's recommended remedy.

by a joint committee of union and employer representatives.

"Under the terms of the agreement, longshoremen registered under the PMA-ILWU contract have first preference of dispatch." A longshoreman who is not so registered is known as a "casual," and may be dispatched for employment if there are no registered longshoremen present, provided he pays his pro rata share of dispatching hall expenses. It is the practice for casual workers seeking employment to telephone for a recorded tape message which indicates whether there is any prospect for employment of casuals on that day. If there is such a prospect, the casuals who telephone may come to the dispatch hall, where available work is assigned out by a dispatcher.

Wilson, Warnken and Thomas were casuals. On August 18, 1964, Wilson complained to William Armstrong, president of Local 12, that the dispatchers were discriminating against them by preferring casuals who were sons of registered longshoremen. These three indicated to Armstrong their intention to picket unless the discrimination was discontinued. Receiving no assurance that the matter would be investigated, they picketed the hall for fifteen minutes on August 19, 1964. They discontinued this when Armstrong assured them that the joint committee would meet with them at 7:30 p.m. on August 21, 1964. The three were present at the time and place set for the meeting, but no meeting was held.

On August 29, 1964, Wilson was put in touch by telephone with W. B. Ferguson, a PMA representa-

tive of the joint committee, who told him to file with
that committee a written statement of grievances.
Wilson, Warnken and Thomas filed such a statement
with the committee later that day. Wilson, Warnken
and Thomas made an oral presentation of their grievances before the joint committee on September 2,
1964. The committee then agreed to take the matter
under consideration and the three casuals stated that
they would abide by the committee's decision. No
action having been taken by September 26, 1964, Wilson, Warnken and Thomas wrote to Ferguson com-
plaining that the situation at the dispatch hall was
much worse. Ferguson wrote back, assuring these
men that the committee was investigating the grievances, and urging them to postpone ". . . any unnecessary drastic action until our efforts have been
expended. . . ."

On October 5, 6 and 7, there were many ships in the
bay and every casual working out of the dispatch hall
was hired except Wilson, Warnken and Thomas.
Rather than dispatch these three casuals, the dispatchers recruited men from taverns and from a
nearby Air Force base to serve the ships then in the
bay.

On October 8, 1964, Thomas and Warnken were at
the hall. Armstrong who was at the hall that day,
testified that these men told other casuals who were
present, "Go on up to the window; there's plenty of
work." They were referring to the small window
through which a prospective casual could talk to a
dispatcher. This was contrary to the dispatcher's

practice of lining up casuals who were at the hall to select those needed for available jobs, rather than to dispatch casuals one at a time through the window.

Joe Jakovac, the relief dispatcher who was then on duty, did not know exactly what Thomas and Warnken were then doing, but testified that he knew that for several days they had been walking around the hall talking to others and trying to start a strike against the hiring procedures. On October 8, 1964, believing that Thomas and Warnken were disrupting established dispatch hall practices, Jakovac stopped the hiring and in the presence of Armstrong, president of Local 12, told them to leave the hall. As they started to leave they met Wilson and told him what Jakovac had said. All three then left. Later the same day, Thomas returned to the hall to talk to Jakovac, but Jakovac told him to ". . . get out and stay out."

Local 12 claimed in the Board proceeding that this eviction was intended to be for that day only. The trial examiner found, however, that in view of the entire context of events, including Jakovac's last statement to Thomas, the eviction was not intended for just one day. The trial examiner also found that Wilson was correct in assuming that he was included in the eviction although Jakovac did not speak directly to him.

The three casuals advised Ferguson of their expulsion from the dispatch hall. Ferguson requested that they take no further action until they heard from him on October 13, 1964. Not having heard from him by that date, Wilson, Warnken and Thomas resumed picketing the dispatch hall the next day and continued to do so until the unfair labor practice charge was filed on October 20, 1964.

The charges came to the attention of the joint committee at a meeting held on October 21, 1964. At that meeting the employer representatives announced that they would have nothing further to do with the matter. The committee has made no disposition of the grievance.

On or about November 13, 1964, a Board representative advised the three casuals to return to the hall and attempt to obtain dispatch to employment. This they did without success.[2]

Based on findings to this general effect, the trial examiner further found that Local 12 discriminated against Wilson, Warnken and Thomas, by refusing to dispatch them when work was available, and by excluding them from the dispatch hall. The reason for such discrimination, the trial examiner found, was to effectuate reprisal for the concerted activities in which these three had engaged. These activities consisted of their concerted protest against Local 12's method of operating the dispatch hall, manifested by picketing the hall, filing a grievance with the joint committee, and making a personal appeal to other

---

[2] Wilson continued reporting to the hiring hall for about fifty days without securing employment. He obtained other employment on February 16, 1965. Warnken regularly went to the hiring hall between November 13, 1964 and March 23, 1965, the date of the hearing in this matter, without being dispatched. Thomas regularly went to the hall between November 13, 1964 and December 4 or 5, 1964, without being dispatched.

casuals present at the dispatch hall on several occasions.

The trial examiner concluded that by reason of the discrimination practiced against these three casuals, Local 12 had committed an unfair labor practice within the meaning of section 8(b)(2) of the Act, by causing or attempting to cause employers to encourage membership in a labor organization in violation of section 8(a)(3) of the Act, 49 Stat. 452, as amended, 29 U.S.C. § 158(a)(3) (1964). Such encouragement, the trial examiner concluded, resulted when the three employees were made aware, through union-motivated discriminatory practices, that they could not expect employment unless they became members of the union and remained in good standing. The trial examiner also concluded that Local 12 committed an unfair labor practice within the meaning of section 8(b)(1)(A) of the Act, by restraining or coercing these three employees in the exercise of rights guaranteed in section 7 of the Act, 49 Stat. 452, as amended, 29 U.S.C. § 157 (1964), particularly the right to engage in concerted activities for the purpose of mutual aid or protection.

In resisting the petition for enforcement, respondent first contests the trial examiner's holding, adopted by the Board, that Local 12 committed an unfair labor practice under section 8(b)(1)(A), by restraining or coercing Wilson, Warnken and Thomas in the exercise of rights guaranteed in section 7 of the Act.

Respondent argues that there is no showing that Wilson, Warnken and Thomas were restrained or coerced with respect to any protected activity. The issue raised by this argument is whether this particular finding of the trial examiner is supported by substantial evidence on the record considered as a whole, this being a proper subject of inquiry in a Board enforcement proceeding. See section (10 (c) of the Act, 49 Stat. 453, 29 U.S.C. § 160(c) 1964).[3]

Before these three casuals manifested their protest by picketing, and by filing a grievance with the joint committee, discriminatory hiring practices were limited to preferring of sons of union members over other casuals. Afterwards, Wilson, Warnken and Thomas were not dispatched at all even when, because of the number of ships in the bay, it was necessary to recruit men from taverns and an Air Force base. When these three men, through concerted activity, sought to call the attention of other casuals present in the dispatch hall to the discriminatory practices, they were ordered out of the dispatch hall. While a dispatcher testified that the exclusion was only intended to be for one day, Wilson, Warnken and Thomas were not so advised by the dispatchers, even when they resumed picketing of the dispatch hall.[4]

[3]In considering that question we are required to apply the rule announced in *Universal Camera Corp. v. N.L.R.B.*, 340 U.S. 474, 488, that the substantiality of the evidence must take into account whatever in the record fairly detracts from its weight.

[4]Respondent argues that these three casuals made themselves unavailable for employment for work from October 8, 1964, when they were barred from the dispatch hall, until November 13, 1964, when they returned to the hall at the suggestion of the Board representative. However, we agree with the trial examiner that after these men were told to get out of the dispatch hall, it was the respondent's responsibility to notify them that the dispatch hall was open to them before it could claim that these men had made themselves unavailable for dispatch.

While the evidence shows that work dropped off substantially in the last quarter of 1964, it is not contended that there was no work for casuals during that period. Respondent argues (citing *Iron Workers Local 433,* 151 NLRB 1092), that where it is not shown that any union representative exhibited hostility to, or resentment against, persons who were not dispatched, it may not be found that such failure was for the purpose of restraining or coercing protected concerted activity. Without passing upon the question of whether a showing of hostility or resentment is indispensable, we believe that hostility and resentment on the part of the dispatchers were demonstrated here. We also think there was a sufficient showing of a specific discriminatory motivation.

Respondent contends that the conduct of Wilson, Warnken and Thomas in the dispatch hall was not protected activity under section 7, pointing to testimony that they were disrupting the operation of the dispatch hall. If the three casuals were disrupting such operations, they should have been advised to this effect and asked to desist. Instead, without explanation, they were ordered to leave. Under these circumstances, they were entitled to assume that they were being excluded because they sought support for their protest against the hiring practices.

Giving application to the rule of *Universal Camera, supra* note 3, we hold that there is substantial evidence supporting the Board finding that, by reason of the described conduct of the dispatchers, Wilson, Warnken and Thomas were restrained in their pro-

tected and concerted effort to protest the discriminatory hiring practices of the North Bend-Coos Bay
dispatch hall.

Respondent next contends that there is no substantial evidence to support the finding of the Board that
Local 12 caused employers to discriminate against
Wilson, Warnken and Thomas, in violation of section
8(b)(2) of the Act.[5] The trial examiner found, in
effect, that such employer discrimination consisted in
withholding employment from these three casuals.
The effect of such discrimination, the trial examiner
could reasonably conclude, was to encourage them to
join the union in order to obtain work assignments.

Respondent argues that there is no evidence in this
record which shows that Local 12 caused or attempted
to cause employers to discriminate against these
three casuals in the manner just described. Again
applying the *Universal Camera* test, we believe there
was ample evidence of this kind. After Wilson, Warnken and Thomas had engaged in concerted activities
in protest against the hiring practices, the employer
discrimination was caused or attempted to be caused
by Local 12 through the simple expedient of not dispatching these men to any of the employers. Respondent is chargeable with knowing that this employer
discrimination, which respondent caused, would tend

---

[5] As noted above, section 8(b)(2) of the Act makes it an unfair
labor practice for a labor organization to cause or attempt to cause
an employer to discriminate against an employer in violation of
section 8(a)(3) of the Act. Section 8(a)(3) prohibits employer
discrimination against employees "to encourage or discourage membership in any labor organization: . . ."

to encourage Wilson, Warnken and Thomas to become union members so that the discrimination would cease.

Respondent also argues that any liability which could arise from the two unfair labor practices discussed above, should not attach to Local 12, but to the International Union, which is not a party to these proceedings. The Board, however, adopted the trial examiner's finding which stated that Local 12 could be held liable for the dispatcher's acts on either a joint venture or an agency theory.

We need not decide whether the trial examiner's joint venture theory has application here because, in any event, the agency theory provides an adequate ground for holding Local 12 liable for the acts of the dispatcher. See *N.L.R.B. v. International Longshoremen's and Warehousemen's Union*, 9 Cir., 210 F.2d 581; *N.L.R.B. v. International Longshoremen's and Warehousemen's Union, Local 10*, 9 Cir., 283 F.2d 558, note 5.

Moreover, since the examiner also properly found that Local 12 was bound directly by the acts of the dispatchers, it could be held responsible for the dispatcher's conduct regardless of whether an agency relationship existed between International and Local 12.

Respondent contended before the trial examiner that it was not responsible for the unlawful operation of the dispatch hall because the hall was under the immediate control of the joint committee, half of whose members were employer representatives associated with PMA. The trial examiner concluded, however, that since Local 12 elected the dispatchers[6] and paid for one-half the cost of maintaining the dispatching hall, it was responsible for the acts of dispatchers whom it selected and paid. This conclusion is consistent with this court's opinion in *N.L.R.B. v. I.L. W.U.*, 9 Cir., 210 F.2d 581, 584.

In addition, Armstrong, president of Local 12, was present when Wilson and Warnken were told to leave the dispatch hall and apparently acquiesced therein. Under this circumstance and the other circumstances discussed above, we are of the view that the trial examiner did not err in concluding that Local 12 could be held responsible for the discrimination which occurred.

Local 12 attacks the provision of the Board order which requires the local to make whole Wilson, Warnken and Thomas from October 5, 1964, for any loss of pay suffered by them as a result of the discrimination of Local 12 against them. The Board order provides that such payment shall be equal to the amount of wages they would have earned but for the discrimination practiced against them, computed on the basis of each separate calendar quarter or portion thereof,

---

[6]Section 8.21 of the 1961-1966 agreement between PMA and ILWU provides that the personnel for each dispatching hall, with the exception of dispatchers, would be appointed by the joint committee. Dispatchers were to be selected by ILWU through elections. In application of these provisions, however, it was the membership of Local 12 which elected the dispatchers.

together with interest at the rate of six per cent per annum.

Local 12 asserts that this back-pay provision is contrary to the holding in *N.L.R.B. v. Local 2, Etc.*, 2 Cir., 360 F.2d 428. In that case, the court modified a Board back-pay order which did not appear to contemplate an inquiry into the length of time the employer would have kept the charging parties at work.

As we read the order here in issue, it contemplates such an inquiry in the compliance proceeding. Such a compliance proceeding usually commences with the issuance, by a Board official, of a back-pay specification. If the answer thereto filed by the respondent presents an issue of fact, a hearing is held before a trial examiner. Therefore, no modification of the order in this regard is needed.

Finally, respondent argues that the proceeding should be remanded to the Board with directions that it consider whether the picketing by Wilson, Warnken and Thomas, and their submission of demands or requests, were protected activities within the meaning of section 7, in view of the fact that the collective bargaining contract contains a no-strike clause and provisions setting up grievance and arbitration procedures.

The no-strike provision of the collective bargaining agreement has no application in this case because the picketing and other activities of Wilson, Warnken and Thomas did not constitute a strike or work stoppage by employees against one or more employers.

See *N.L.R.B. v. Illinois Bell Telephone Co.*, 7 Cir., 189 F.2d 124, 127; *THE POINT REYES*, 5 Cir., 110 F.2d 608, 609-610; *C. G. Conn, Ltd., v. N.L.R.B.*, 7 Cir., 108 F.2d 390, 397.

The question of the availability of the grievance procedure is not properly before us. Insofar as the record before us indicates, the only objection which respondent made before the agency with reference to whether respondent had restrained or coerced Wilson, Warnken and Thomas in engaging in a protected activity, had to do with their activity within the dispatch hall in seeking to enlist the support of other casuals. As to this particular occurrence, respondent's only contention was that the activity was not protected because it involved a disruption of the dispatch hall—not because alternative grievance procedures were available.

Since the argument which respondent now advances was not the basis of any objection made in the agency proceeding, it is not available to respondent in this court. See section 10(e) of the Act, 49 Stat. 454, 29 U.S.C. § 160(e) (1964); *N.L.R.B. v. Cheney California Lumber Co.*, 327 U.S. 385, 387-388; *N.L.R.B. v. International Ass'n of Machinists, Lodge 942, AFL-CIO*, 9 Cir., 263 F.2d 796, 798.

The petition will be enforced.

As amended by order of May 18, 1967.

Appendix "B"

United States Court of Appeals
For the Ninth Circuit

National Labor Relations Board,
                                    Petitioner,

vs.

International Longshoremen's and Ware-
    housemen's Union, Local No. 12,
                                    Respondent.

No. 20,914

DECREE

Before: Chambers and Hamley, Circuit Judges, and
    Byrne, District Judge.

This Cause came on to be heard upon the petition
of the National Labor Relations Board for the enforcement of a certain order issued by it against the
Respondent, International Longshoremen's & Warehousemen's Union, Local No. 12, its officers, agents,
and representatives, on November 18, 1965. The
Court heard argument of respective counsel on December 14, 1966, and has considered the briefs and
transcript of record filed in this cause. On April 18,
1967, the Court being fully advised in the premises,
handed down its decision granting enforcement of the
Board's order. In conformity therewith, it is hereby

Ordered, Adjudged and Decreed by the United
States Court of Appeals for the Ninth Circuit that

International Longshoremen's & Warehousemen's Union, Local No. 12, North Bend-Coos Bay, Oregon, its officers, agents, and representatives shall:

A. Cease and desist from:

(1) Discriminating in the hire and tenure of employment of Donald Wilson, Lee Thomas and Bernard Warnken, by failing and refusing to dispatch them to work by reason of the protected concerted activities engaged in by said individuals.

(2) In any other like manner interfering with, restraining or coercing Donald Wilson, Lee Thomas and Bernard Warnken in the exercise of their rights guaranteed by Section 7 of the Act, except to the extent that such right may be affected by an agreement made in accordance with the provisions of Section 8 (a)(3) of the Act requiring membership in a union as a condition of employment.

B. Take the following affirmative action which the Board has found will effectuate the policies of the National Labor Relations Act, as amended (hereinafter called the Act).

(1) Make whole Donald Wilson, Lee Thomas and Bernard Warnken in the manner specified in the portion of the Decision of the Trial Examiner entitled "The remedy" for any loss of pay suffered by them as a result of the discrimination of International Longshoremen's & Warehousemen's Union, Local No. 12 against them.

(2) Notify the Joint Port Labor Relations Committee of North Bend-Coos Bay and the dispatchers

of the hiring hall in that area, and furnish copies of such notices to Wilson, Warnken and Thomas, that Wilson, Warnken and Thomas will have full use of this hiring hall without discrimination in connection with their dispatch to employment.

(3) Notify the above-named individuals if presently serving in the Armed Forces of the United States of their right to full use of this hiring hall without discrimination in connection with their dispatch to employment, upon application in accordance with the Selective Service Act and the Universal Military Training and Service Act of 1948, as amended, after discharge from the Armed Forces.

(4) Upon request make available to the National Labor Relations Board or its agents for examination and copying all payroll records, social security payment records, timecards, personnel records and reports and all or any other records necessary for the determination of the amount of backpay due under the terms of this Decree.

(5) Post in conspicuous places in its offices and in the North Bend-Coos Bay hiring hall, including all places where notices to employees or members are customarily posted, copies of the notice attached hereto and marked Appendix A. Copies of this notice shall, after being duly signed, be posted immediately upon receipt thereof, and maintained for a period of 60 consecutive days thereafter. Reasonable steps shall be taken by the Respondent Union to insure that said notices are not altered, defaced or covered by any other material.

xviii

(6)   Notify the said Regional Director, in writing, within 10 days from the date of this Decree, what steps the Respondent has taken to comply herewith. Endorsed, Decree Filed and Entered

/s/   William B. Luck
     William B. Luck
          Clerk

[A True Copy
Attest:

          William B. Luck
               Clerk]

Appendix "C"

The relevant provisions of the National Labor Relations Act, as amended (61 Stat. 136, 73 Stat. 519, 29 U.S.C., Secs. 151, et seq.) are as follows:

Sec. 7. Employees shall have the right to self-organization, to form, join, or assist labor organizations, to bargain collectively through representatives of their own choosing, and to engage in other concerted activities for the purpose of collective bargaining or other mutual aid or protection, and shall also have the right to refrain from any or all of such activities except to the extent that such right may be affected by an agreement requiring membership in a labor organization as a condition of employment as authorized in section 8(a) (3).

Sec. 8 (a)   It shall be an unfair labor practice for an employer—

(1)   to interfere with, restrain, or coerce employees in the exercise of the rights guaranteed in section 7;

*　*　*　*

(3)   by discrimination in regard to hire or tenure of employment or any term or condition of employment to encourage or discourage membership in any labor organization:

*　*　*　*

(b)   It shall be an unfair labor practice for a labor organization or its agents—

(1)   to restrain or coerce (A) employees in the exercise of the rights guaranteed in section 7 . . .

(2) to cause or attempt to cause an employer to discriminate against an employee in violation of subsection (a) (3) . . .

* * * *

Sec. 9 (a) Representatives designated or selected for the purposes of collective bargaining by the majority of the employees in a unit appropriate for such purposes, shall be the exclusive representatives of all the employees in such unit for the purposes of collective bargaining in respect to rates of pay, wages, hours of employment, or other conditions of employment: Provided, That any individual employee or a group of employees shall have the right at any time to present grievances to their employer and to have such grievances adjusted, without the intervention of the bargaining representative, as long as the adjustment is not inconsistent with the terms of a collective-bargaining contract or agreement then in effect: Provided, further, That the bargaining representative has been given opportunity to be present at such adjustment.

* * * *

Sec. 10(a) The Board is empowered, as hereinafter provided, to prevent any person from engaging in any unfair labor practice (listed in section 8) affecting commerce. This power shall not be affected by any other means of adjustment or prevention that has been or may be established by agreement, law, or otherwise: * * *

(b) Whenever it is charged that any person has engaged in or is engaging in any such unfair labor practice, the Board, or any agent or agency designated by the Board for such purposes, shall have power to issue and cause to be served upon such person a complaint stating the charges in that respect, and containing a notice of hearing ... .

* * * *

(c) * * * If upon the preponderance of the testimony taken the Board shall be of the opinion that any person named in the complaint has engaged in or is engaging in any such unfair labor practice, then the Board shall state its findings of fact and shall issue and cause to be served on such person an order requiring such person to cease and desist from such unfair labor practice and to take such affirmative action including reinstatement of employees with or without back pay, as well as effectuate the policies of this Act; * * *

* * * *

(e) The Board shall have power to petition any court of appeals of the United States * * * for the enforcement of such order * * * and shall file in the court the record in the proceedings, as provided in section 2112 of title 28, United States Code. Upon the filing of such petition, the court shall cause notice thereof to be served upon such person, and thereupon shall have jurisdiction of the proceeding and of the question determined therein, and shall have power to * * * to make and enter a decree enforcing, modifying, and enforcing as so modified, or setting aside in whole or in part the order of the Board. No objection that has not been urged before the Board, its member, agent, or agency, shall be considered by the court, unless the failure or neglect to urge such objection shall be excused because of extraordinary circumstances. The findings of the Board with respect to questions of fact if supported by substantial evidence on the record considered as a whole shall be conclusive. * * * Upon the filing of the record with it, the jurisdiction of the court shall be exclusive and its judgment and decree shall be final, except that the same shall be subject to review by the * * * Supreme Court of the United States upon writ of certiorari or certification as provided in section 1254 of title 28.

* * * *

Office-Supreme Court, U.S.
F I L E D

AUG 29 1967

JOHN F. DAVIS, CLERK

No. 447

In the Supreme Court of the United States

OCTOBER TERM, 1967

INTERNATIONAL LONGSHOREMEN'S AND
WAREHOUSEMEN'S UNION, LOCAL 12, PETITIONER

v.

NATIONAL LABOR RELATIONS BOARD

*ON PETITION FOR A WRIT OF CERTIORARI TO THE
UNITED STATES COURT OF APPEALS FOR THE
NINTH CIRCUIT*

BRIEF FOR THE NATIONAL LABOR RELATIONS BOARD IN OPPOSITION

THURGOOD MARSHALL,
Solicitor General,
Department of Justice,
Washington, D. C. 20530.

ARNOLD ORDMAN,
General Counsel,

DOMINICK L. MANOLI,
Associate General Counsel,

NORTON J. COME,
Assistant General Counsel,

WILLIAM WACHTER,
Attorney,
National Labor Relations Board,
Washington, D.C., 20570.

INDEX

CITATIONS

Cases:

Cases—Continued
Page

In the Supreme Court of the United States

OCTOBER TERM, 1967

No. 447

INTERNATIONAL LONGSHOREMEN'S AND
WAREHOUSEMEN'S UNION, LOCAL 12, PETITIONER

v.

NATIONAL LABOR RELATIONS BOARD

---

*ON PETITION FOR A WRIT OF CERTIORARI TO THE
UNITED STATES COURT OF APPEALS FOR THE
NINTH CIRCUIT*

BRIEF FOR THE NATIONAL LABOR RELATIONS BOARD IN OPPOSITION

OPINIONS BELOW

The opinion of the court of appeals (Pet. App. i-xiv) is not yet officially reported. The Board's Decision and Order (R. 35-36, 18-30)[1] are reported at 155 NLRB 1042.

---

[1] "R." refers to "Volume I, Pleadings"; "Tr." refers to the stenographic transcript of the unfair practice hearing; "G.C. Exh." refers to exhibits of the NLRB's General Counsel; "U.Exh." refers to the Union's exhibits. These documents comprised the record in the court of appeals, and certified copies thereof have been filed with the petition.

(1)

JURISDICTION

The decree of the court of appeals (Pet. App. xv-xviii) was entered on May 9, 1967, and a petition for rehearing was denied on May 18, 1967. The petition for a writ of certiorari was filed on August 2, 1967. The jurisdiction of this Court is invoked under 28 U.S.C. 1254(1).

QUESTION PRESENTED

Whether substantial evidence supports the Board's finding that petitioner Union violated Section 8(b)(2) and (1)(A) of the Act, by refusing to dispatch employees to jobs as longshoremen and barring them from the dispatching hall because they engaged in a protest against the Union's dispatching procedures.

STATUTE INVOLVED

The relevant provisions of the National Labor Relations Act, as amended (61 Stat. 136, 73 Stat. 519, 29 U.S.C. 151, *et seq.*), are set forth in Appendix C to the petition, at pp. xix-xxii.

STATEMENT

A. The Facts

In 1961, the International Longshoremen's and Warehousemen's Union ("ILWU") and the Pacific Maritime Association ("PMA") entered into a five-year collective bargaining agreement providing, *inter alia*, for the dispatching of longshoremen to jobs through halls operated jointly by ILWU and PMA

(R. 20, 18; U. Exh. 2, pp. 1, 42, Tr. 7, 11). Under the terms of the agreement, grievances relating to the operation of the halls were to be adjusted by Joint Port Labor Relations Committees ("Joint Committees") composed of an equal number of ILWU and PMA representatives (R. 20; U.Exh. 2, pp. 43, 64). Petitioner Union ("Local 12") is the local affiliate of ILWU in the port of North Bend-Coos Bay, Oregon (R. 20; Tr. 166). Local 12 selects the dispatchers for the North Bend-Coos Bay hall and pays for one half of the hall's operating expenses. (R. 21; Tr. 35-37, 77, 101, 119, 167.)

Bernard Warnken, Donald Wilson and Lee Thomas worked in North Bend-Coos Bay port as "casual" longshoremen, that is, non-registered longshoremen who are dispatched to jobs when no registered longshoremen are available (R. 20; Tr. 15, 12). On August 18, 1964, Wilson and Bernard Warnken's brother Bill complained to Local 12 President Armstrong that the dispatchers at the local hall were discriminating against them by preferring sons of registered longshoremen (R. 21; Tr. 167, 101, 119, 77, 35-37). On the following day, Wilson and the Warnken brothers picketed the hall until Armstrong promised that the Coos Bay Joint Committee would meet with them at 7:30 p.m. on August 21. When they arrived at the designated time and place, however, no members of the Joint Committee appeared (R. 21; Tr. 101, 119, 97).

On August 29, Wilson and Bernard Warnken protested to a PMA representative on the Joint Committee and were told to file a written statement of

4

grievances with the Committee which they did later that day (R. 21; Tr. 43, 50, 84, 86, 103; G. E. Exh. 4). Their statement assailed the "unjust system" of favoring sons of registered longshoremen and complained that the method of selection used by the relief dispatcher, Joe Jakovac, made the casuals "feel * * * like a sheep being herded out to pasture" (R. 21; G.C. Exh. 4). On September 2, Wilson, Warnken and Thomas orally presented their grievances to the Joint Committee (R. 21; Tr. 77, 103, 138, 83). No action had been taken by September 26, when they complained to a PMA representative that the "situation * * * has gotten worse" in that they were being "froze out altogether," and suggested that they were about to take "further actions" (R. 21; G.C. Exh. 3, Tr. 78, 90, 138). The PMA representative asked them to "allay any unnecessary drastic action until our efforts have been expended * * *" (G.C. Exh. 5).

On October 5, 6, and 7, every casual at the hall was hired except Wilson, Warnken and Thomas. Additional casuals were even recruited from taverns and a nearby Air Force base (R. 21; Tr. 57, 105-108, 111). On October 8, in Union President Armstrong's presence, dispatcher Jakovac evicted Warnken, Wilson and Thomas from the hall, stating that "[t]his is a private hall and we've got the right to ask anyone to leave here that we don't want" (R. 21; Tr. 111, 125-126, 137, 170-173). The three men then left. When Thomas returned to the hall later that day, Jakovac told him to "get out and stay out" (R. 22; Tr. 127-138).

Wilson then protested to a PMA representative, who promised that they would hear from him on the following Tuesday, October 13. That Tuesday, the three men "waited all day [at Wilson's home] and never heard a word" (R. 23; Tr. 59-60). The following day, October 14, they resumed picketing the hall and continued to picket until October 20, when they filed an unfair labor practice charge with the Board (R. 21; G.C. Exh. 1(a), 60, 71-72, 113, 128). At a meeting of the Joint Committee on October 21, the charges came to the attention of the members, whereupon the employer representatives announced that they would have nothing further to do with the matter. The Committee made no disposition of the grievance. (R. 24; Tr. 72, 91, 140.)

Wilson, Warnken and Thomas did not enter the hall again until November 13, after a Board agent advised them that the Union had alleged that their expulsion from the hall was for one day only (R. 23; Tr. 122-123, 113, 128-129). Between that time and March 23, 1965, Warnken reported to the hall some 90 mornings without being dispatched to a single job (R. 23; Tr. 113-114, 104, 121, 60-61). Wilson reported for about 50 days without being dispatched, and finally obtained other employment on February 16, 1965 (R. 23; Tr. 60-64, 78-79, 51-52). Thomas reported regularly between November 13 and December 4 or 5 but received no work (R. 23; Tr. 130, 60-61). Other casuals, with earnings comparable to theirs during the first three quarters of 1964, continued to be referred to jobs at approximately the same rate during the final quarter of 1964 and the first two months of 1965 (R. 23; G.C. Exh. 2, Tr. 14-15). With one exception, casuals were dispatched to work every weekly payroll period between September 29, 1964 and March 8, 1965 (G.C. Exh. 2).

B. The Decision of the Board and the Court of Appeals

Upon the foregoing facts, the Board found (R. 26-27, 29) that Local 12, through the conduct of the dispatchers, had violated Section 8(b)(2) and (1)(A) of the Act, by refusing to refer Warnken, Wilson and Thomas to available jobs and barring them from the hall because they had picketed and filed grievances to protest the dispatching procedures. The Board ordered the Union, *inter alia*, to cease and desist from the unfair labor practices found and to make the three employees whole for any loss of pay suffered by them as a result of its unlawful conduct (R. 29-31, 35-36).

The court of appeals sustained the Board's findings and enforced its order (Pet. App. i-xiv).

ARGUMENT

The decision of the court of appeals, which turns on its special facts, is correct and not in conflict with the decision of any other court of appeals. There is no occasion for further review.

1. It is well settled that a union violates Section 8(b)(2) and (1)(A) of the Act if, in the administration of an otherwise lawful hiring arrangement, it refuses to refer an applicant for employment in order to retaliate against him for challenging the union's

policies or the conduct of its agents. *Lummus Co.* v. *National Labor Relations Board*, 339 F. 2d 728, 734 (C.A. D.C.); *National Labor Relations Board* v. *Local 138, Operating Engineers*, 293 F. 2d 187, 193 (C.A. 2); *National Labor Relations Board v. H.K. Ferguson Co.*, 337 F. 2d 205, 207-208 (C.A. 5), certiorari denied, 380 U.S. 912. Petitioner Union's principal contentions (Pet. 8-11, 13-15), that Warnken, Wilson and Thomas were not denied any available employment and were only asked to leave the dispatch hall for causing a "disruption," merely raise "substantial evidence" questions, which do not warrant review by this Court. *Universal Camera Corp.* v. *National Labor Relations Board*, 340 U.S. 474, 490-491; *National Labor Relations Board* v. *Pittsburgh Steamship Co.*, 340 U.S. 498, 502-503.

Moreover, petitioner's claim that the loss of work which these three men suffered resulted solely from their alleged disruption of activities in the union hall flies in the face of the record which shows that they had been denied work on the three days prior to the alleged disruption and that after they returned to the hall in November, 1964, they were totally excluded from work. The record amply supports the findings of the Board, sustained by the court of appeals, that this exclusion from employment was a direct result of "reprisals directed by the dispatcher against them * * * motivated by their concerted specific objections to the method of hiring * * *." (R. 27).[2]

---

[2] Similarly unsupported is the Union's contention (Pet. 10-11) that it did not cause any employer to encourage union

8

2. There is no merit to petitioner's argument (Pet. 15-17), that the Board's order should be modified to expressly state that backpay liability must be determined on the basis of the actual number of days the employees would have been employed but for the discrimination. As the court below held (Pet. App. xiii), the Board's order already "contemplate[s] an inquiry into the length of time the employer would have kept the charging parties at work"; it provides (R. 29, 30) that the Union should make them whole "for any loss of pay suffered by them as a result of the [Union's] discrimination" and "payment shall be equal to the amount of wages they would have earned but for the discrimination practiced against them. . . ." *National Labor Relations Board* v. *Local 2, United Ass'n of Journeymen, etc.*, 360 F. 2d 428 (C.A. 2), is inapposite. There the Board required the union to make the employees whole for all loss of pay resulting from their lack of employment during a specific period coinciding with the union's discrimination, even though the employees had never "demonstrated their employability, since they were never put to work." *Id.*, at 434. Here the Board provided back

membership by discrimination, within the meaning of Section 8(b)(2) of the Act. As the Board and court below held (R. 28, Pet. App. x-xi), the Union caused employer discrimination "through the simple expedient of not dispatching these men to any of the employers" and this tended "to encourage union membership in that it was designed to compel adherence to union policy in the operation of the hiring hall." See *Radio Officers' Union* v. *National Labor Relations Board*, 347 U.S. 17, 28-33, 39-42, 50-52. Nor was the Board, as the Union contends (Pet. 11-12), required to issue a complaint against the employers as well as the Union. *Id.*, at 53-54.

9

pay only for the period the casuals would have worked "but for the [Union's] discrimination * * * against them."

3. The Union cannot fairly urge (Pet. 17-20) that Wilson, Warnken and Thomas had no protected right to "picket in protest against an employer's hiring policy in the face of a grievance procedure through which such issues could be raised." For, as the Board and court below found (R. 27, Pet. App. vi-x), the Union discriminated against the casuals not only because they picketed but also because they invoked the very grievance machinery upon which the Union now relies.[3] In any event, as the court of appeals further held (Pet. App. xiv), the Union raised no such objection before the Board (R. 32-34) and is thus precluded by Section 10(e) of the Act from doing so now. *Marshall Field & Co.* v. *National Labor Relations Board*, 318 U.S. 253, 255-256; *National Labor Relations Board* v. *Seven-Up Bottling Co.*, 344 U.S. 344, 350; *National Labor Relations Board* v. *International Union of Operating Engineers, Local 66*, 357 F. 2d 841, 846 (C.A. 3), and cases cited, n. 10.

---

[3] *National Labor Relations Board* v. *Tanner Motor Livery*, 349 F. 2d 1 (C.A. 9), relied on by the Union (Pet. 15, 18, 20), is inapposite, since there the court simply remanded the case to the Board to determine whether an employer could discharge employees protesting his racially discriminatory hiring practices "when there is an established collective bargaining representative having a contract with the employer and the employees do not act or seek to act through that representative." *Id.*, at 3.

CONCLUSION

The petition for a writ of certiorari should be denied.

Respectfully submitted.

THURGOOD MARSHALL,
Solicitor General.

ARNOLD ORDMAN,
General Counsel,

DOMINICK L. MANOLI,
Associate General Counsel,

NORTON J. COME,
Assistant General Counsel,

WILLIAM WACHTER,
Attorney,
National Labor Relations Board.

AUGUST 1967.

CPSIA information can be obtained
at www.ICGtesting.com
Printed in the USA
BVHW081110121118
532890BV00010B/497/P

9 781270 557371